AMAZON FIRE HD 8 WITH ALEXA

Advanced Amazon Fire HD Manual to Help You Use Amazon Fire HD 8 with Alexa Like a Pro in 2017

By Paul Weber

© Copyright 2017 – Paul Weber – All rights reserved.

In no way is it legal to reproduce, duplicate, or transmit any part of this document by either electronic means or in printed format. Recording of this publication is strictly prohibited, and any storage of this material is not allowed unless with written permission from the publisher. All rights reserved.

The information provided herein is stated to be truthful and consistent, in that any liability, regarding inattention or otherwise, by any usage or abuse of any policies, processes, or directions contained within is the solitary and complete responsibility of the recipient reader. Under no circumstances will any legal liability or blame be held against the publisher for any reparation, damages, or monetary loss due to the information herein, either directly or indirectly. Respective authors own all copyrights not held by the publisher.

Legal Notice:
This book is copyright protected. This is only for personal use. You cannot amend, distribute, sell, use, quote or paraphrase any part or the content within this book without the consent of the author or copyright owner. Legal action will be pursued if this is breached.

Disclaimer Notice:
Please note the information contained within this document is for educational and entertainment purposes only. Every attempt has been made to provide accurate, up to date and reliable, complete information. No warranties of any kind are expressed or implied. Readers acknowledge that the author is not engaging in the rendering of legal, financial, medical or professional advice.

By reading this document, the reader agrees that under no circumstances are we responsible for any losses, direct or indirect, which are incurred as a result of the use of information contained within this document, including, but not limited to, —errors, omissions, or inaccuracies.

Table Of Contents

Chapter 1: What is the Fire HD 8 With Alexa 6
    Specifications 7
    Operating system 7

Chapter 2: How to Set Up your Fire HD 8 With Alexa 9
    Connecting to Wi-Fi 9
    Registering 9
    Completing Setup 10

Chapter 3: Navigation 12
    How To Create A Calendar Event 13
    Installing Google Play 14

Chapter 4: Alexa 19
    Using Alexa 19
    What Can You Do With Alexa? 20
    Alexa's Features 22
    Lists 24
    Alarms 25
    Smart Devices 25
    Skills 26
    Using Silk 27

Chapter 5: Reading On the Fire HD 29
    Media 29
    Audiobooks 31

Conclusion 33

Chapter 1: What is the Fire HD 8 With Alexa

Amazon has proven that Alexa, the Amazon assistant is very helpful. However, many people wondered how well Alexa would work on the Fire HD 8 tablet because it is not always listening like the Echo or the Dot.

The Fire HD 8 is the very first tablet that includes Alexa. Instead of yelling "Alexa," as you are walking through your house, you simply hold down the home button on the Fire HD 8. This means that you do have an extra step to take when you are accessing Alexa however, this could be a good thing.

How many stories have we heard of lately of people's children saying something and Alexa ending up ordering something outrageous like a huge dollhouse or 30 pounds of cookies? So if you have wanted to use Alexa as your assistant but have been a bit afraid of having an Echo in your home due to stories such as these, the Fire HD 8 tablet may be the answer.

Alexa does make the Fire HD 8 tablet a much more capable device than other tablets so it is worth not being able to access Alexa simply by speaking.

Of course, besides pressing a button instead of speaking out "Alexa," Alexa works exactly the same as it does on the Echo devices. You will be able to use all of the same voice commands that you are used to using with Echo devices and you are going to be able to run most of the skills as well. Of course, you will still be able to run all of your smart devices from your Fire HD 8 just as you would an Echo device.

The Fire HD tablet will be used differently than the Echo devices though. It is very easy for you to ask Alexa about the weather forecast, or to turn on the lights, however, it is a bit different when you are cooking for example and your hands are covered in food. You don't want to reach over and touch your Fire HD. It is times like this that the Echo devices do come in handy.

It is understandable that Amazon would not have Alexa be voice activated on the Fire HD 8 because it is a tablet. If Alexa was voice activated, the battery would drain very quickly.

Specifications

8-inch screen (1280X800 pixels)
HD display with over 1 million pixels
1.5 GB of RAM
Quad-core 1.3 GHz processor
The choice of 16 or 32 GB of storage as well as the ability to expand the storage up to 200 GB by using a microSD.
12-hour battery
According to tests, the Fire HD 8 is 2 times as durable as the iPad.
720p HD Camera that is front and rear facing that records 1080p videos
Unlimited storage on the cloud for all of your pictures
Dolby Audio immersive speakers as well as a built-in microphone
On Deck for prime members which allows you to download the first episodes for Amazon Originals.

Operating system

The operating system is called Fire OS 5 Bellini. This operating system according to Amazon has hundreds of improvements when compared to previous versions and there are additional features as well.

The company used Android Lollipop as the base for Fire OS however, they then customized the operating system so that it is integrated with the Amazon network as well as the Amazon cloud service.

This operating system provides an improved entertainment experience giving the Amazon devices the look of a magazine. A new speed reading feature was also introduced with Fire OS 5 Bellini called Word Runner. Word Runner is supposed to help you to improve how fast you read and it does so by presenting only one word at a time in the center of your screen. According to Amazon, this helps the reader by bringing the focus to the word. The program also learns the pace that you read and it also slows down when more complex words are used.

Chapter 2: How to Set Up your Fire HD 8 With Alexa

When you receive your Kindle Fire HD 8, you are going to take it out of the box and get to using it right away, however, you will not be able to do this if you do not know how to set it up. When you turn the Fire HD 8 on for the first time, you are going to find that there are several screens that you need to go through in order to set up and register your tablet. Don't worry though, there are not a lot of questions and they are very easy for you to answer.

Connecting to Wi-Fi

The first thing that you are going to want to do is to connect to a wifi network. You will find on the first screen a list of the available networks for you to connect to. If you have an open wifi network, you will not have to have a password, however, if you do have a closed network, you will have to enter your password.

Once you connect to the internet, you will then be taken to the register screen.

Registering

Once you connect to a wifi network, you will need to register your device. In order to do this, you will simply enter the information that is associated with your Amazon account. You will need your email address that is associated with the Amazon account as well as your Amazon account password.

If you do not have an account with Amazon you will click on the "New to Amazon" link in order to create an account. This link is automatically going to take you to a screen where you can enter your name, email, and a password, creating a new Amazon account.

After you have entered your information you will then tap the "continue" button to move to the next screen.

On the next screen, you are going to be asked to agree to the terms. Make sure that you click on the link and actually read the terms. After you have read the terms, close them and you will be taken back to the registration screen. Press the 'register' button.

Completing Setup

The next screen that you are going to be taken to is the "Select Your Timezone," screen. It is important for you to make sure that you choose the correct time zone. If you do not choose the correct time zone, your time will not be correct on your tablet and this is going to cause a few different issues.

Of course, if you set any alarms or try to use your calendar to schedule appointments, the time is going to be wrong. The bigger issue, however, comes with connecting to your wifi network. If the time on the device is not the same as the time on your wifi network, you may find that you cannot connect.

If you are located outside of the United States, you are going to need to tap 'more' and then choose your time zone. Once you select your time zone, you will press the back button which is located on the bottom of the screen on the left corner. This is then going to return you to the "Select Your Time Zone" screen.

Another screen is going to appear which will ask that you confirm your account. You will press the 'continue' button. There is also going to be a link that will have your name in it. If you are not that person, for example, if you have accidentally entered the wrong information and someone else's name shows up, tap the "not (name)" and change accounts.

Once this is done, you will be taken to a screen where you can choose to connect to your social networks. All you have to do is to tap on the social media icon and sign into your account in order to connect to it.

When this is done, or if you do not want to connect to any social media sites, you will press "Get Started Now."

The next screen is going to be the first in a series which is meant to help you learn about the features that are included with the tablet as well as how to use some of the important ones. You will tap the "Next" button which is located in the middle of the screen on the right-hand side in order to navigate through the screens.

When you are finished navigating through the screens, you will press the 'close' button. This will take you to the Kindle Fire HD 8 home screen.

Chapter 3: Navigation

Working through the setup of the Fire HD 8 will help you learn a bit about navigating using the touchscreen. The navigation of the touchscreen works like most touchscreen devices. However, if you have never used a touchscreen device before, or if you just want a refresher course, here are a few tips:

1. When you are on the home screen, swipe down from the top of the screen where the status bar is located. This is going to display Quick Settings. You can then choose what setting you want to go to or swipe up to hide the settings.

2. In order to open an app, simply tap the icon.

3. Your Fire HD 8 can go to the lock screen after it has not been used for a period of time. In order to go begin using the Fire HD 8 once again, you will place your finger on the unlock button and then swipe from right to left. There is also a special offers button which you can place your finger on and swipe from left to right if you would like to check out the latest offers from Amazon.

When you are on the ad screen, if you want to go back to the home screen, simply tap the home button. The home button is in the shape of a tiny house.

4. If you need to enlarge the text on the screen, simply double tap the screen. If you want to return the text to the normal size simply tap the screen a third time. This feature is only going to work when you are using certain apps. When you are using other apps, such as when you are reading a book, if you double tap the screen the tools will be displayed.

If you are using an app where tapping the screen does not enlarge the text, simply put two fingers on the screen and then move them apart to zoom in. In order to return the screen to the normal size, put your thumb and finger on the screen and tweak them together.

5. When you are using an app that involves going from one page to the next like the e-reader, simply swipe your finger from the right to the left in order to go to the next page. In order go back, you will place your finger on the screen and swipe it to the right.

6. When you are scrolling up or down a web page, simply swipe your finger up or down the screen depending on which direction on the page you want to go.

Using these techniques will allow you to get around the screens and navigate your Fire HD 8.

How To Create A Calendar Event

When you use the Fire HD 8's calendar app, your events are going to be synced with whatever calendar you choose to use however, you can also add events from your Fire HD 8.

Begin by tapping on the date in which you want to add the event. A new event screen will pop up. Press the plus sign. The form for the new event is then going to appear on the screen. Fill out the form with the information about the event.

You will begin by tapping on the area that says "new event." This is where you are going to type the name of the event.

Next, you will tap on the time located to the right of 'From'. You will then place the time that the event will begin in this area. On the right of 'To,' you will place the time that the vent will end.

You can skip this step and tap on the box next to 'all day' if the event is going to take all day.

Next, you will decide if you are going to place this event on your calendar in regular intervals. You can do this by tapping on 'repeat.' You can then choose weekly or monthly. This is good when it comes to specific events that you know are going to take place on a regular basis. You will simply add the event once and it will continue to appear on your calendar as needed.

Now you can choose whether or not you want to create a reminder. All you have to do to create a reminder is to tap on 'reminder'.

You can also invite those that you have saved as contacts if you want them to join you at the event.

Then you will choose 'save.' Once you save the event, it will appear on your calendar.

Installing Google Play

The Fire HD 8 is going to restrict you to only using the Amazon app store, however, because it runs on an operating system which is based on Android, you will be able to install

Google Play Store and then have access to all of the android apps.

The great thing about this is that it does not even require you to do rooting which can void your warranty. After you follow the steps that I am going to give you, you will be able to access the Play Store in about half of an hour or less.

There are two different ways for you to install Google Play on your Fire HD8. The first option is a bit easier, however, because not all methods will work for everyone, I am including two. This way, if you have trouble with one option you can use the other.

Option 1-
Begin by going to your settings and then choosing security. Choose to enable apps from unknown sources. This is going to allow you to install the APK files that will allow you to access Google Play.

Next, you are going to go to the silk browser and use the following 4 links to download the APK files that you need.

http://www.apkmirror.com/apk/google-inc/google-account-manager/google-account-manager-5-1-1743759-release/google-account-manager-5-1-1743759-android-apk-download/

http://www.apkmirror.com/apk/google-inc/google-services-framework/google-services-framework-5-1-1743759-release/google-services-framework-5-1-1743759-android-apk-download/

http://www.apkmirror.com/apk/google-inc/google-play-services/google-play-services-9-8-77-release/google-play-services-9-8-77-230-135396225-android-apk-download/

http://www.apkmirror.com/apk/google-inc/google-play-store/google-play-store-7-0-25-h-all-0-release/google-play-store-7-0-25-h-0-android-apk-download/

In order to download each of the files, simply follow the link, scroll down the screen and then choose "Download APK."

When the download starts, there will be a pop-up appear. The pop-up is going to tell you that the file could be harmful to your device. Tap OK and don't worry the file will not harm your device.

Continue to do this for all 4 files.

Once you have downloaded all 4 files, close the silk browser. Next, open up your file manager. It is labeled "Docs" Go to 'local storage." Then choose 'downloads.' The four files that you downloaded will be in the download file. Tap one at a time in order to install them. Make sure that you open than in the order that they were downloaded which should be the same order that they are listed in.

Once you click one of the files, you will be taken to the next screen where you will choose install which is located at the bottom of the page. Repeat this for each of the files.

Once you are done installing all of the files, the Play Store app is going to appear on your home screen. Tap on the icon and you can then sign in using your Google account.

The Play Store may not work perfectly right after you install it, however, if you give it a bit of time (sometimes as long as 10 minutes) it will update and run normally. Now you can search for whatever app you want to use.

Option 2-

If you find that option 1 does not work for you for some reason then you can try option two which is a bit more complex but works.

In order to use this potion, you are going to need a PC as well as a USB cable. There should have been a USB cable included when you received your Fire HD 8 and it will work perfectly fine.

First, you will go to the settings on your Fire HD 8 and choose 'device options' which is located under the device option. Find the serial number and then tap on that field repeatedly. It may take more than 7 taps but soon it will show 'developer options.' Chose the 'developer options'.

Next, scroll down until you see 'enable ADB.' Tap it in order to enable it. Normally this is a feature that only developers use so you are going to have a warning pop up and you will have to agree to that warning if you want to continue with this option.

After you have enabled the ADB, use your USB cable to connect the Fire HD 8 to your PC. Windows will detect that you have connected the device and the necessary drivers will then be downloaded.

Once the drivers are downloaded, you will go to http://rootjunkysdl.com/?device=Amazon%20Fire%205th%20gen&tag=823814-20 on your PC and then download Amazon-Fire-5th-Gen-Install-Play-Store.zip". Unzip the file after it is downloaded and then open the 1-Install-Play-Store.bat in order to get started.

On your Fire HD, you will see a pop-up that says, "Allow USB debugging?" Choose 'OK.'

When this begins it will go to the first screen where you will type the number 2 and then press enter. This will allow the tool to know that you want it to install the Play Store.

The app will then be installed on your Fire HD 8. Once this is done, you are going to be asked to reboot your tablet. Do so by tapping okay. Unplug the USB cable from your PC and tablet. Go back and disable the option 'Enable ADB' as well if desired.

You will find the Play Store app on your home screen. You can then tap on the app and log in using your Google account. Just as with the previous option, the app may not run properly at first but it will update itself in about 10 minutes and run normally.

Chapter 4: Alexa

The Echo made Alexa one of the most popular virtual assistants out there. Alexa can help you with everything from scheduling appointments to checking the traffic conditions to turning your lights off in your home. It is the perfect virtual assistant for everyone out there and everyone can find a use for Alexa.

Alexa is the Amazon version of Siri and is available for use on the Fire HD 8. Alexa on the Fire HD 8 is a bit different than on the Echo devices because Alexa is not always listening. When you use one of the Echo devices, Alexa listens for you to say the trigger word. However, when you use Alexa on the tablet you do have to press the button.

As mentioned earlier, having Alexa listen all of the time could be a bit problematic therefore ensuring that you have to press a button to activate Alexa could actually work in your favor.

Another great feature that the Fire HD 9 offers that the Echo does not is the screen. Since the Fire HD 8 does offer a screen, Alexa is now able to show you any relevant information that pertains to the question that you have asked.

Using Alexa

Alexa is able to do all of the basic tasks as soon as soon as you take your Fire HD out of the box. This means that as soon as you sign in, you can begin asking for Alexa to look up facts or complete conversions.

Once you have sat up our Fire HD 8 you will be able to visit Alexa.amazon.com in order to start adding skills which we will talk a bit more about later.

The initial version of Alexa does have a few limitations. You are going to have to enable 'always on' when you first launch Alexa.

In order to activate Alexa, you will tap and then hold the home icon on your Fire HD screen. The home icon looks like a tiny house. Once Alexa 'wakes up' you will say your command. You do not have to say "Alexa" as you do when you are using one of the Echo devices.

One of the great things about having Alexa right on your tablet is that she can go wherever you go which means she is always available for you to use as long as you have access to wifi.

Of course, you should not expect Alexa to perform as she does no the Echo devices. For example, you can ask Alexa to play Christmas music, while Alexa will play Christmas music it may take about 30 seconds for it to start. On the other hand, when you use an Echo device the music starts immediately.

What Can You Do With Alexa?

Alexa is great when it comes to making sure that you have all of the timers that you need. All you have to do is tell Alexa to set a time for a specific amount of time. If you need to know how much time is left on your time, all you have to do is ask Alexa. This ensures that if for example, you have a kitchen timer set, you can go into another room and work on something else without having to worry about missing the timer and burning your food.

Alexa also allows you to order items off of Amazon without ever having to visit the website. If you notice you are running out of diapers, just tell Alexa to order more. You will see a picture of the item and then Alexa is going to ask you if this is the item that you want to buy. This does give people some peace of mind in knowing that Alexa is not going to order the wrong item.

When you use Alexa on the Echo devices you can ask about the weather but when you use Alexa on the Fire HD 8, you can see the weather forecast. When you ask Alexa about the weather, a weather card is going to appear on your screen. You can then scroll down the card and see all of the weather information for the entire week. It is much like the information that you would get if you were to run a weather app.

You can use the Automatic Voice Cast to find out what is happening on your Echo device. For example, you can check to see what music someone is listening to and so forth. While this is not an extremely helpful feature it is interesting.

Of course, the tablet with Alexa is going to play music or update you on the news whenever you ask but Alexa will also let you listen to podcasts. If the podcast is available on TuneIn, Alexa will play it on demand. If you want a different episode from the latest, you will have to do this manually though.

Alexa on your Fire HD 8 will be able to turn out the lights just as if she would on the Echo devices. We will talk more about the smart devices such as lights that Alexa can control a bit later.

Alexa's Features

In order to activate Alexa on the Fire HD 8, you will tap and then hold down the home icon until a blue line appears on your screen. When you see the blue line you can ask your question or give your command.

When answering a question, Alexa may provide you with a visual. In order to exit the visual, simply press the back button and the visual will be removed from your screen.

You can turn Alexa on or off by swiping down from the top of your screen. Once the quick settings are open you will choose settings, then device options then Alexa. When you tap Alexa you will turn the virtual assistant on or off.

If you have the parental controls enabled on the Fire HD 8, Alexa is going to be automatically disabled. Alexa will also be disabled on any child profiles.

You can listen to media and music by telling Alexa to play it for you. For example, you can tell Alexa to 'Read (and then the title of a book)' or 'Play (and then the name of a song)'. When Alexa is reading a book the text is not going to appear on the screen.

When Alexa is playing music or reading a book, the controls are going to be on the screen so you can pause the music or book.

Alexa will also allow you to play videos as well. You can ask Alexa to find a certain movie or a television show. You can also ask Alexa to show you movies that have a certain actor that plays in them or that are a specific genre.

Of course, Alexa can provide you with the answers to your questions, the news, the weather, and the traffic conditions.

Alexa can also help you to update your calendar. You are able to link your supported calendar to Alexa via the app. Once you do this you will be able to ask Alexa about any upcoming events as well as use Alexa to add new events. You can link one calendar from each of the supported calendars, for example, Apple, Google, and Microsoft Office 365.

In order to link your calendar, you will first launch your Alexa app. You will then go to the menu and choose settings. Next, choose the calendar. Find your calendar account in the list of providers. Click on the calendar that you want to use and then choose link. You will then simply follow the instructions that are on the screen which will then allow Alexa access to that calendar.

You will have to provide your login information for the calendar that you choose to use and then allow Alexa to access the calendar.

Once you link the account you will be asked which calendar you want to use, for example, work, home, etc.

When this is done you can use Alexa to access the calendar. In order to find out when your next event is you can ask Alexa, "What is next on my calendar?" You can also ask, "What is on my calendar on Tuesday?" Or even ask about a specific time on a specific day.

If you want to add an event to the calendar you will say, "Add an event to the calendar." Alexa will then help you add the event. In order to delete an event simply say, "Delete (and name the event) from my calendar."

Lists

You will also be able to access your lists via the Alexa app. In order to make a new list, you will say, "Create a new list." Alexa will ask you what you want the name of the list to be. After you confirm the name of the list you can begin adding items to the list.

If you want to create a list using the Alexa app, you will go to the app, then select the menu and choose lists. Next, you will choose create list and manually type in the name of your list. Select the + icon and you can start adding to your list.

If you want to rename the list, simply choose the area that is located in the front of the name of the list and then choose the pencil icon. You can then type in the new name. In order to archive a list, find the list and then tap the arrow that is in front of the name of the list. Tap on archive list.

If you want to delete a list you will go to view archives and then find the list that you want to delete and tap, delete list.

You can manage your lists by saying, "Add (and then the name of the item) to (the name of the list.) Or you can ask Alexa what is on a specific list by saying, "What is on my (and then the name of the list) list?

If you ask Alexa to email you the list, she can do that as well.

Alarms

In order to set an alarm, all you have to do is say, "Set alarm for (then the time that you want the alarm to go off.) You can create a repeating alarm by telling Alexa to set a repeating alarm for (whatever day of the week and the specific time.)

After you create an alarm you can go into the Alexa app and edit it. You will from the menu choose timers & alarms. Then you will go to the alarms tab and choose the alarm that you want to edit. From here you can choose to have the alarm repeat daily, on weekdays, on weekends, on specific days of the week and you can also delete the alarm. Once you have made your changes you will tap save changes.

Smart Devices

Before you begin you will want to enable your smart home device skill. We will talk about skills next. However, before you enable the skill, make sure that you read the safety information about using smart devices with Alexa.

Next, you need to make sure that your smart device will work with Alexa. You will follow the manufacturer's directions to set up the device, connecting it to the same wifi network that Alexa is connected to. Once this is done you will go to your Alexa app link Alexa with the device. You will download as well as install any updates for the device.

In order to connect your device to Alexa, you will go to the Alexa app. Then you will tap on skills. You can from here, either browse the devices or type in keywords related to your device in order to find the right skill. Next, you will tap enable.

If you cannot find a skill for your device, the device may not be compatible. After you enable the skill you will follow the directions on your screen in order to link the device with Alexa. Then you will tell Alexa to discover your device. Or you can go to the smart home section using your Alexa app and simply tap add device.

Skills

A skill is nothing more than the Alexa version of an app. You can use skills on the Echo devices as well as on your Fire HD 8 or any device that uses Alexa. As of right now, there are over 8,000 different skills that can be used with Alexa so you are sure to find exactly what you are looking for. If not, don't worry, there are new skills launched almost every day.

Once you add a skill to your account, you will be able to use it on all of the devices that are connected in your home. The skills make Alexa even more helpful.

Skills are not features. A feature is embedded into a tablet or other device. The skill is a third-party app which you will add to Alexa in much the same way as you would add an app to your phone. There are skills that focus on news, such as The BBC News skill, skills for social media, and thousands of others.

When you add a skill to Alexa you will find that there are many different benefits. First of all, you are going to be able to use Alexa to perform tasks using that skill. You can also use these skills to create a smart home which will allow you to view the next room via the camera that is connected, control the temperature, turn on the lights and so much more.

The skills will help make your life easier and that is exactly what Alexa is supposed to do.

Using Silk

Silk is the internet browser that is used on Amazon devices. Amazon did not use an existing browser because having their own browser allows their customers the fastest experience.

In order to use silk, you will begin at the home screen. If you are not on the home screen, tap the home icon. Next, you will tap the web icon which will take you directly to Silk. If you want to display the address bar, simply swipe down from just below the status bar.

On the bottom of the screen, you will find an options bar. The options bar includes a back and forward icon, a search icon, and an icon which will allow you to enter the site address via the onscreen keyboard.

You can display more than one page at a time by using taps. If you want to add a tab, simply tap the + icon in the top right corner of your screen. When you do this you will see thumbnails of sites that you have recently visited. Tap on the thumbnail of the site that you want to go to or tap the address bar and type in the site's address.

Silk will allow you to bookmark sites just like other browsers will. Bookmarking a site is going to allow you to find them quickly when you are looking for them.

In order to add a bookmark all you have to do is swipe down from the top of the screen just below the status bar. Then you will tap the bookmark icon which is located to the left of the address bar and looks like a ribbon.

If you want to delete the bookmark, hold your finger on the page until a menu appears. On that menu, you will choose delete. A dialog box will then appear confirming that you want to delete the bookmark and all you have to do is choose OK.

Chapter 5: Reading On the Fire HD

When you tap the books icon on your home screen you will be taken to your books library. The library is going to contain all of the content that you have downloaded under the device tab. The content that is located on the cloud will be found under the cloud tab.

The tab which you are using will appear orange. You will also see a store button which if tapped will take you to Amazon so that you can get more books.

If you tap the menu button you will be able to choose how you want your books displayed. You can choose grid or list. You can also choose how you will sort your titles by pressing the buttons located near the top of the screen. You can choose by author, by recent, or by title.

You can determine which titles have been recently downloaded because they will have a small banner in the corner of each thumbnail. The banner will read, "New."

In order to read a book, all you have to do is tap on the book that you want to read.

Media

It is likely that you are going to want to copy some of your media files to your tablet from your PC or to your PC from your tablet. This is a very simple process to do. You will connect your Fire HD 8 to your PC via the USB cable which comes with the Fire HD 8.

Then you will open the file manager on your PC and find the drive that is named 'Fire.' Open Fire. In this drive, you will see that there are many different files. Some are videos, books, pictures, music, and documents. This is where you are going to drop the media from your Pc.

Find whatever file you want to copy on your PC, right-click it and then choose copy. Go back to the Fire folder that you want to drop the media in and right click on that file. Choose paste. Of course, you can also drag the file and drop it where you want it to go.

You will do the same thing when moving files from your Fire HD 8 to your PC. When you are done make sure that you choose disconnect and then unplug the USB cable.

You can also launch subscription-based services such as Netflix, Hulu, and Amazon Instant videos. If you want to buy movies, television shows or books on the Fire HD 8 you will want to make sure that you have a wifi connection, an Amazon account, as well as a credit card associated with your Amazon account.

Once you do this it only takes a few seconds for you to choose what media you would like to purchase.

If you are an Amazon Prime member you can stream your movies and television shows to your Fire HD 8. There is unlimited streaming offered however you can also purchase movies and television shows. It is the most popular titles that you will need to purchase.

In order to watch the video, you will tap on the video icon, then the word store. Tap on the title that you want to watch and then you will choose to either rent or purchase the movie or television show.

If you plan on being offline for a while it is a good idea for you to download the video instead of stream it. That way you can watch it whenever you want.

Listening to music is also an option. You can copy music from your PC or you can purchase it from Amazon. You can go to the Amazon music library and access all of the music that you have previously purchased.

order to play a song or an album, simply tap on the song or um. You can do other things on the Fire HD 8 while the c is playing such as reading or browsing the internet. In to do this, you just have to tap the square 'overview' icon h from one app to the next.

A oks

One o   ures of the Fire HD 8 is the ability for you to listen t he Audible Audiobooks. You will find that there is a dedicated app just for audiobooks. If you do not have an Audible account you will be given an introductory offer.

You can purchase the audiobooks by tapping on the audiobook that you want to read and then choosing 'buy.' There are different Audible plans that will allow you to download a different number of audiobooks each month.

In order to play that audiobook, you will go to your library and the find the book that you want to listen to. Tap the play icon and start listening. It is important for you to make sure that the Fire HD 8 is connected to a wifi network or to download the book if you know that you are not going to have access to wifi for a while.

You can also change the Audible settings by opening the menu and then choosing settings. You can improve the sound of the books by choosing High-Quality Format. You can also choose to enable push notifications. It is also possible for you to change how far you want the audiobooks to jump when going forward and back. The default setting is 30 seconds. In order to change this setting, you will tap on the jump forward/back option and then determine how long you want the setting to be. You can choose anything from 10 seconds to 90 seconds.

Conclusion

The Fire HD 8 with Alexa is an amazing tablet that is going to help you do all of the things that you want to do on one simple device. The tablet is very easy to use. It can double as your personal assistant, keep your organized, provide entertainment for you and your children all day long, and it can even help turn your home into a smart home by controlling your smart devices.

Spend some time exploring your Fire HD 8 and get to know it. There are so many different features that I would never be able to cover them in this book.

This book is a simple guidebook to help you navigate your Fire HD 8. Of course, there are thousands of different skills that you can add to your Fire HD 8 which will make it that much more useful for you. There really is nothing that this amazing tablet cannot do.

I hope that this book has provided you with some helpful information and that it has helped you to learn all about your Fire HD 8.

Check Out My Another Books

Fire Stick: Amazon Fire TV Stick Guide to Help You Install Kodi on Your Fire Stick & Immerse You into The World of Your Media

Amazon Echo Show: Advanced Amazon Echo Show Guide to Help You Use Echo Show Like a Pro & Enrich Your Smart Home

Amazon Echo Dot: Advanced Amazon Echo User Guide to Help You Use Amazon Echo Dot in 2017 & Enrich Your Smart Home

Printed in Poland
by Amazon Fulfillment
Poland Sp. z o.o., Wrocław